The Taco Boat

Other Works by Al Ortolani

Slow Stirring Spoon (chapbook), High/Coo Press, 1981

The Last Hippie of Camp 50, Woodley Press, 1989

Finding the Edge, Woodley Press, 2011

Wren's House, Coal City Press, 2012

Cooking Chili on the Day of the Dead, Aldrich Press, 2013

Waving Mustard in Surrender, NYQ Books, 2014

Francis Shoots Pool at Chubb's Bar, Spartan Press, 2015

Paper Birds Don't Fly, NYQ Books, 2015

Ghost Sign (co-authored), 39 West Press, 2016

How Wally Lost His Thumb and the Boy Scouts Became Cannibals, Spartan Press, 2018

On the Chicopee Spur, NYQ Books, 2018

Hansel & Gretel Get the Word on the Street (chapbook), Rattle Press, 2019

Swimming Shelter: An Exercise in 100 Days of Poetry, Spartan Press, 2020

The Taco Boat

Poems

Al Ortolani

The New York Quarterly Foundation, Inc.
Beacon, New York

NYQ Books™ is an imprint of The New York Quarterly Foundation, Inc.

The New York Quarterly Foundation, Inc.
P. O. Box 470
Beacon, NY 10508

www.nyq.org

Copyright © 2022 by Al Ortolani

All rights reserved. No part of this book may be used or reproduced in any manner whatsoever without written permission of the author except in the case of brief quotations embodied in critical articles and reviews.

First Edition

Set in New Baskerville

Layout by Raymond P. Hammond

Cover Design by Raymond P. Hammond

Cover Painting: "Smokey Joe", acrylic on canvas, 20 x 16" © 2011 by Jacque Allen Forsher | www.jacqueforsher.com

Library of Congress Control Number: 2022946280

ISBN: 978-1-63045-089-2

The Taco Boat

Contents

Author's Note x

orange juice sucked dry

The Taco Boat 15
Smudge Pots 16
Mexicans Cutting Trees 17
Saturday at the Pawn Shop 18
Watching the Lunar Landing on Television while Taking
   Tickets at the Drive-In Theater 19
I Make a Joke about Equanimity at the Waffle House 20
The Senate Vows Impartial Justice 22
Stopping at Blackjack Camp after the Veteran's Writing
   Workshop 23

crumbs on his belly

DNA 27
Carp 28
One-Star Toenail 29
What We Keep 30
Signature Piece 31
No Phil Rizzuto 32
Socrates Played Second Base 33
The Lovely Mechanic 34
Choosing the Five-Year Battery 35
Butterfly Valve 36

a nut job steps into the fast food

Grandma Goes Heavy 39
Keeping the Stetson 40
Death of the Machinist's Mate 41
Topeka Tornado 1966 42
Of an Evening 43
Five-Dollar Horn 44

Thump *45*
Alley Window *46*

a six cent Green River

Dogs Have Changed *51*
The Antique Cheeseburger *52*
Stand-Up Cat *53*
Owner's Manual *54*
Polio Turtle *55*
Tying Flies *56*

Jell-O kingpins

Billy Collins Pisses Me Off *59*
Caught Naked with Her *60*
Visiting the Retina Specialist *61*
Pharmacy Run *62*
Morning Feathers *63*
Guilt Trip *64*
Alf Chooses the Cherry Pie *65*
Alf Considers the Next Big Thing *66*
Alf Works the South Hallway *67*
We Were English Majors Once *68*
Watching the Solar Eclipse in the Rain *69*
My Brother and I Break Dance at Another
Family Wedding *70*

up to his knuckles in Kimchee

Abbey Raises Chickens *73*
General Tso's Chicken *74*
Chickens Are Still Chickens *75*
In Search of Quivira We Found Chicken Fried Rice *76*
Peeing at McDonald's after Eating a Chicken Sandwich ... *77*
Suffering on the Floor of a Fast Food Bathroom Stall I
Imagine Amerigo Vespucci in Japan *78*

Biscuit Boy 80
Drinking with the Governor 81
Nearly Poor White People 82

eats rarely, sinks like a rock

The Used Bookstore Buys More than a Papercut 85
Whitman as Coyote 86
The Potted Sonnet 87
A Life Jacket for Oliver 88
Wild Geese 89
The Argument 90

Xanax and coffee latte

Bad Eye 93
slicing the five o'clock cake 94
cleaning the inbox 95
First Walk in the Rain after Retirement 96
Dust Jacket 97
Interrupting the Artist 98
Walking under September Pines 99
Good Friday 100
Sleeping in Railroad Cave 101
The Calico Mayor 102
Flying Over the Coast of Greenland 103
Moving the Elks Club Piano 104
At the Home for Imbecilic Youth 105
Green Tara 106

a small goat smothered in salsa

Goats Unbidden 109
Ashes 110
Creeping South 111
Taking the Chipmunk Seriously 112

Cow Creek Snow ... *113*
Goldfinch Burial ... *114*
Before It's Too Late ... *115*
Memorial Day Weekend ... *116*
Writing a Love Poem while the Plumber Snakes
the Basement Drain ... *117*
Cabin in the Woods ... *118*

he nibbled at my gloved hand

Raising the Ladder ... *121*
November Faces ... *122*
High Ceilings ... *123*
Coffee Tonight ... *124*
Weekenders ... *125*
I Have Never Known a Hummingbird to Drink
to Excess ... *126*

after smashing peanuts

Cucumbers ... *131*
Growing Tomatoes ... *132*
Two Truths about Fishing ... *133*
The Sleep of Emmett Kelly ... *134*
Cigar Box ... *135*

Acknowledgements ... *137*

Author's Note

I'd like to give a special thanks to my friend and former student Jacque Forsher of Dallas, Texas, for her cover art, and to H.C. Palmer, Jimmy Pappas, and Alexis Rhone Fancher for providing comments that capture the spirit of *The Taco Boat*. A special thanks goes to Raymond Hammond and NYQ Books for believing in my poems enough to publish this book. Finally, to my wife, Sherri, my children, and grandchildren, without whom I'd be living in a small van down by the river with the squirrels and muskrats, and to Stanley our soul-dog, *woof.*

for Sherri

orange juice sucked dry

The Taco Boat

Last night, I bought a 12-pack of tacos
at Taco Bell, not because I was
especially hungry, but because I could.
My ship had come in, you see,
and for once, I was rolling in it.
I ate six of them in front of the television
while bingeing on episodes
of some Netflix series, not because
it was particularly engaging, but simply
because I could. My ship, if you recall,
had come in. I packed up the other six tacos
and brought them to work for lunch
where my fellow employees marveled,
or laughed, I couldn't tell which, at
my ability to eat six soggy tortillas,
microwaved in their wrappers, and spread
like dollar bills on the table. I gave
one to a friend, and she was happy,
happy for the taco, happy for me,
happy for everyone who waited
for a boat, any boat, to come in.

Smudge Pots

I've seen smudge pots at auctions,
blackened by decades of smoke.
Usually, they're lined
in back near the dog pen
with the rusted shovels, double-
bladed axes, sledges, and piles
of rebar. I once met a retired farrier
who collected anvils, and a farmer
who kept his living room
hung with hay hooks and barbed wire.
Somewhere there's a collector
of smudge pots. Greased
with layers of soot, he knows
their intricacies, the makes
and models, the refinements
of the high end from the low end.
He remembers the merits of smudge,
edging the lonely highway
or thwarting the killing freeze,
the orchards, the dead man's curve.
He lights them still, keeps an old can
of kerosene in the garage.

Mexicans Cutting Trees

They pile branches in a long row
from their high-power chipper
to the next driveway, the top climber
in a long sleeve t-shirt, trailing rope

and carabineers, walks to the back
of the truck and opens a compartment
next to the wheel well. He moves slowly
from his day in the branches, pitched

above the rooftops of Greenway Lane.
He drops his seat harness
and stuffs it in a bin with webbing
and good rope. A sign on the truck reads,

Keeping America Beautiful.
They start up the chipper and feed
fresh, suburban poplars, maples, elms
into its whirring teeth.

Saturday at the Pawn Shop

The shop owner's heart condition
stops him in the middle of the aisle
back behind the glass counter of pawned
wedding rings and petite tennis bracelets.
He holds himself, hands out for balance,
head swimming in some cloud
of sale and resale, pawn slips, overdue
notices, promises to come back soon.
It's all I have worth something,
this diamond, this handgun.
I thought better to sell, than not eat.
The spell passes and he lowers his arms,
breathes again. Last time he fell,
crashed behind the counter, the EMTs
had to move the glass case, shake up
the rows of hope, the lineup of rings
and Lugers. Better to fall here among
the power tools, the abandoned drills,
the orbital sanders, the heap of tightly
wound electrical cords, better the air
compressors and the chop saws
than the jewelry, the wall of guitars,
the Gibsons, the Fenders, the Martins
that never learned to play themselves.

Watching the Lunar Landing on Television while Taking Tickets at the Drive-In Theater

There was suspicion at the front gate
that below the bug-riddled marquee
nothing could change Kansas,
not the moon dust, not the pock-marked
Sea of Tranquility, not the cheese
that wasn't cheese.
Crickets chirred in the weeds
like they had for thousands of years,
the moon floated, and we wondered
about the coming true of things,
sitting back in our lawn chairs
to see the great distance we'd come.
One car, a Buick maybe, rolled in
from the highway, headlights
bright in our eyes. The driver,
obviously drunk, raised two fingers
for two tickets, the peroxide blonde,
pressed against his fleshy bicep, sipped
whiskey from a Dixie cup. She leaned
over his lap to see,
blinking her mascaraed lashes
at the television, and then again
at the moon overhead.

I Make a Joke about Equanimity at the Waffle House

The waitress behind the counter
asked if there was anything
she could get me, my plate
of eggs mopped with toast,
the orange juice sucked dry
through a straw. I told her, only
inner peace. She didn't pause,
kept her ballpoint scratching out
my addition. She tore the bill
from her pad. Squared me up
with both eyes. Inner peace
is hard to give, she
        tapped her pen
without sarcasm. Her bar cloth
sponged a ring of water
from under my glass. For me,
it's more like being born
in the wrong century. Something
about 1900 appeals to my nature.
Times were slower, I add.
Simpler. I'm not naive,
she went on. My grandma
worked her ass off. Grandpa
died before I came along.
She turned the water on
at the wash station, began
sinking a load of cups,
        saucers, egg plates.
I sure as hell wouldn't want
to be pumping water
from a well. But all this
having, and not having, she
motioned to 75th Street,
is just too much. The door
opens with the first

lunch traffic. She shows them
the good booth. She clicks
her tongue, points her finger at me
like a loaded pistol. Somewhere,
her grandmother listens
to Jimmy Rodgers, his blue yodel
unwinding on a Victrola,
a wobble of wrens
in the cotton of a curtain.

The Senate Vows Impartial Justice

Sheltered from the ice, a bird
has taken cover
in the Christmas wreath,
forgotten below the porchlight.
This evening I use the backdoor,
slipping across the lawn,
around the frozen forsythia,
and then down the driveway
like a skater. I don't need
to move a muscle. Gravity
does the telling as I slide
to the mailbox.
It is shellacked with ice,
glazed in the gray dusk.
I smack the metal lid
with my fist, and a hundred webs
crack the glossy sheen.
I walk the lawn up to the house,
the weight of junk mail
in my hand. I plant each step.
Blades of grass shatter,
give way to my heel.
If I walk the front steps, the bird,
some midwestern species,
maybe a sparrow, a starling,
will fly into the cold, rather
than risk my approach.
No amount of coaxing
will keep him nested
against the siding. No promise
will keep him hidden
in pine needles. He has learned
nothing from my words,
my concern for falling mercury,
the frozen night.

Stopping at Blackjack Camp after the Veteran's Writing Workshop

October is full of small burials,
between the white oaks, the hickory,
the cottonwood. Along Captain's
Creek, the single birdsong, the constant
cricket, are airborne with yellowed leaves.
The undergrowth of bedstraw and briar
tangles my feet; burdock and cocklebur
snag my jacket, burrow into my boot laces.
Like Velcro they ride the Santa Fe's
wagon swale into John Brown's battlefield
where years before Harper's Ferry
the first bullets found flesh. I slap them
from my pant legs, this Kansas,
seed after seed into the open earth.

crumbs on his belly

DNA

He's always been good to us
was a line my mother used
when referring to someone the family
could rely on. Her words

elevated them to an ally,
like the optometrist
who took payments for
eyeglasses, a little a month
squeezed out of my father's
teaching salary, or the owner
of the grocery store on Joplin Street
who ran an account,
paid once a month when the check
came in. It was a poor person's line,
a reference of respect to those
who didn't hold their position
like a clipboard of overdue slips,
or rustle a sheaf of eviction notices.

My mother's people were Irish,
forced from Kerry to Appalachia, then
from Kentucky to Missouri, finally,
scattering in Ancestry.com files.
The line was engrained in her DNA.
Field after field, they set
the plow-turned stones
in fences with narrow stiles.

Carp

Their relationship was one-sided,
of course, the fish did little
except swim peaceful circles
around the edge of the bowl.
He'd mastered the small window
of his life. She tried not to over
feed him, a sure death the pet
store owner warned. Fish will
eat whether they are hungry
or not. Her first husband was
similar. He grubbed
the kitchen cabinets for chips
dribbled crumbs on his belly
into the cushions of the couch.
She wearied over vacuuming,
brushing Lays and Cheetos
from the bottoms of her feet.
When she complained, he suggested
she wear shoes. The goldfish was
simpler, his mess contained
in colored pebbles, his slow journey
around the bowl expected.
Once a month, she'd put him
in a coffee cup with a dipper of water
and drain the bowl. She rinsed
the pebbles under the tap, which
she had to admit were rank.
Opening the window, lighting
a sandal wood candle,
took less effort than stuffing
laundry into the Maytag,
the bubbles the fish
kissed against the glass
nearly a greeting.

One-Star Toenail

No window in my room
except for the one
to the ventilation shaft.
The curtain moves to the wind
of an interior breeze. White stucco
on the opposite wall, irregular,
cracks like freshets, creeks,
rivers to the sea.

Using a fingernail clipper
and paper clip,
I pry an in-grown toenail
out of my big toe.
One of these days
I'll pay a doctor. For now
I am a thousand miles
from home. Ventilation fans
suck the blue from the sky,
drown the cries of seagulls
as they circle and snap
at taco shells and gluten-free
hot dog buns. My eyes,
(windows themselves I'm told)
water from the strain
of cataract, glaucoma,
and smart phone screen.
Like a yoga master,
I pull my foot
inches from nose.

What We Keep

I consider myself lucky to sit today
at an old desk, window open,
the soft whirr of the brass-bladed Emerson
fluttering the pages of a paperback.
On the wall is a photograph (1909)
of my grandmother, age 3 or 4, staring
quizzically into the lens, sister
and cousins of similar ages, caught
at the feet of their grandparents.
A quilt hangs as a backdrop
from the porch of their Ozark home.
My uncle once said that he knew
where the quilt was stored, but that was
years ago. Even more time has passed,
my uncle gone, his children
as old as grandparents themselves,
the quilt in a chest somewhere, or not.

Signature Piece

I wander through her rooms
in this little cat piss house,
searching for something over-
looked by the early morning
pickers. There is an odd
assortment of cheap Native
American prints, a few from
unknown artists, others from
flea markets and garage sales.
An Edison Victrola, cylinder
style, has been hacked up
with parts that don't belong.
The old furniture is labeled
Eastlake, but that's not true
either. The carpet in the main
room has been removed (cat
piss) so I walk on the glue-smeared
concrete that cracks under
my shoes. A bedroom
in the back of the house is so
over-powering that I can't enter,
blankets, bedspread, pillows
still in place. The cat room
someone says, skipping out
into the hallway, nose-covered,
a bronze lion under an arm.

No Phil Rizzuto

My father was anesthetized
by television, his gout-swollen foot
raised on a pillow. We'd lean over
his shoulder, careful not to bump
the recliner, baseball cards
spread like a poker hand.
He'd thumb through them
for us, tap his finger on one.
This guy was a bum, a bush leaguer,
couldn't buy a hit. Now here,
he taps again, was a good glove,
no Phil Rizzuto, but soft hands
with the hot potato. Then he'd
hand the cards back
over his shoulder, and we knew
enough was enough, eyes shut, heart
pulsing in his toe, a working man
with a king's disease.
Gary Cooper on the television
squared off in *High Noon*,
white hat, pearled six shooters,
steady legs to walk up the street
into the arms of Grace Kelly.

Socrates Played Second Base

Royals' pitchers have begun to shift
their launch point towards the center
of the rubber. In theory, it gives them

control over the low, outside fastball,
the down and out, which is nearly impossible
to hit. The fastball is a batter favorite

when the ball rises belt high, centered
like a ripe melon, a fat apple, a cheese moon.
Even the little guy, swinging out of his shoe-

laces, prefers the four-seamer, straight
and true as a fact. Baseball is a bit Socratic,
Know Thyself between the lines.

The barefoot old Greek in the second-hand toga,
chatters questions like a little leaguer,
pops the dust from his glove.

The Lovely Mechanic

After hours, the mechanic
who changed my oil
comes to my house in the icy
night and says she forgot to put
the test plug (not the drain plug)
back in the top of my rear
axle. She holds up
a rachet and a piece of metal
wrapped in a red shop rag.
I'm sorry. I need to put it back
where it should have been.
I didn't notice until you'd gone
it was sitting on the bench.
Didn't you get my phone call?
I left this message you see, but
I'm here anyway to right the wrong
and she crawled under my truck
with a flashlight and a socket,
her legs stranded on the driveway
like those of a corpse, but bent
a little to the right so she could
better see. She kept apologizing
for the screw up, insisting I
come in tomorrow so they could
recheck the fluid level. That's
when she shouted—false alarm. Plug
in place. She wormed from under
the truck back into the cold.
I'm really sorry, she insisted,
for bothering you. It's a plug
of mistaken identity—
she was happy. I was happy,
both of us shivering on the porch
an hour past closing.

Choosing the Five-Year Battery

Woke mid-morning during a rainstorm. I took the Rav4 into the *Lyle's Fix It* for a battery replacement. Nearly two hundred dollars later, I'm back home at the computer, wondering how any of this could have been so expensive. I double check the work order, the receipt. At first, I'm not really seeing it in battery cables. However, the automotive guy, Lyle's assistant, did tell me some interesting stories about his ex-wife's post partem depression. His divorce papers said, she didn't care enough to care. My eyes teared up. Kind of heavy for *Lyle's Fix It* while replacing the Rav4 battery, even if it was the five-year variety. I seem to bring that out in people, sad stories leak all over me like antifreeze through a loose ring clamp. Maybe I just like to watch the wrench turn, the simplicity of clean terminals, the foreverness of a five-year decision. I take comfort in the extra turn on a troublesome nut.

Butterfly Valve

Wiring the exhaust pipe
to the frame of the truck
is a skill I learned from my father.
He could keep a piece of shit
Ford or Chevy or Plymouth
running without repairs
longer than anyone I knew.
It was kind of a gift to himself,
keeping cash from the mechanic
for as long as possible. He'd
make do with a leaking gas tank
by not topping it off, or avoid
a 60 mile per hour
front end shimmy by driving 55.
As his children moved away
into lives of their own, the money
ran more freely. He gave up
lying on the street with
his shoulders wedged under
the chassis. He scheduled
regular automobile check-ups
where he'd sit out in the shop
with the wrench turners
and tell stories about how
he used to keep his junkers
running with bailing wire, heated
with cardboard in front
of the radiator, ignited with ether,
a screwdriver wedged
in the throat of the carburetor.

a nut job steps into the fast food

Grandma Goes Heavy

My best friend bought a Glock
which he keeps in a locking case
in his bedroom. He and his petite wife
are considering a license for concealed
carry. She's so small, so light boned,
I wonder where she'll tuck it, bulging
from the small of her back, or under
an arm she can't lower. I suppose
a handbag will do, the pistol
wedged next to her checkbook,
lipstick, mascara. Even so, I doubt
she'll pull it in an emergency. She isn't
one to dig through her purse when
a nut job steps into the fast food,
his rage so many shades
of colored pencils.
Who prepares for madness?
She has grandkids-in-tow below the table,
the handbag rifled next
to the chicken nuggets,
honey mustard, spilled ketchup.

Keeping the Stetson

Aunt Dorothy, widowed for much
of her adult life, kept her husband's hat
in the back window of her gold
Oldsmobile. It failed in the sunlight
to keep her from loneliness
on the weekly trip to the IGA, but
saved her (she insisted) from the mashers
(her word), the carjackers, the stalker
who might follow her home
to an empty house. Leaving a man's hat
in the back of the car made sense
to her, a widow's comfort,
as plumb as a locked door, almost
like having a husband at the hardware store
buying a dead bolt and a chain latch.

Death of the Machinist's Mate

Today, we found
a photograph in the
woodshop, young sailors
with collars unbuttoned, smiling
into the lens at Pearl
like tomorrow was as given
as sunrise. Your grin
was easy to spot,
thumb-tacked to the shop wall,
behind the clamps,
the wood glue, the spar
varnish. You seldom
spoke of the Navy, except
to laugh how boats
made you seasick. The heavy
lathe, the calibrated saws,
the drill press, moored
like silent ships.
Decades of sawdust
hid in the crevices
of the wall joists, the gaps
between the floorboards
that the broom could
not touch.

Topeka Tornado 1966

I was taken by the apartments
split open like doll houses, rooms still
populated with furniture, beds unmade,
blankets and sheets tossed, end tables
with shaded lamps, framed pictures
cock-eyed on flowered wallpaper. We drove
the streets in our scoutmaster's car,
following the tornado's path,
pointing into bedrooms, into closets,
like pigeons without windowsills—
a bathtub, fastened to a drain, hung
from a second story, a roll
of white paper fluttered,
a mirror reflected our Chevrolet.
I was embarrassed for them,
the poor, the homeless
with their lives turned out to see
the secrets in cabinets,
the underwear on the floor,
the stain on the bed.
In the sun that shouldn't
be shining, in the crooked lines
the wind wouldn't take,
a cat crouched back up the stairs.

Of an Evening

the neighbors sit in the summer heat,
waiting for the air to cool.
The first bug zapper in town
hangs on a pole under the shadow
of a tree. The yard flickers like a foreign film
that I don't understand. I want to jump
the curb into their circle, not
to small talk, since I don't know
how to speak to adults, nor to drink beer,
since that's against the rules, but just
to witness the purple explosions.
Violet colors my chrome wheels, splays
my spokes, feathers my legs.
There is a tingle to the floating dust
that draws me to them, a union
of forces, baritone-throated men,
bell-voiced women, stories punctuated by
exclamations, the bright poof.

Five-Dollar Horn

During the time between wars,
my father took trumpet lessons
in a studio perched
above the Coca Cola sign
in Times Square. He rode the train
from Huntington with his trumpet
secure in its fake alligator case.

Harry James was blasting the clubs
in Harlem. The Huntington boys
stood at the door, rocking on their heels.
Dad grew a pencil-thin moustache, wore
a blue jacket, a loosened tie. Every Friday
he soloed at the all-school assembly.
Once he sat in with the Long Island Symphony.
Even after Korea,
he blew smoky improvisations

alone in our basement. At length,
he passed his five-dollar horn
to his son for grade school band,
but I was embarrassed by the ratty case, the dents,
the lack of shine on its antique bell.
Surrounded by sparkling Conns and Reveres,
I learned to clear the spit valve,
bleated in last chair, favored the mute.

Thump

The job involved stapling sheets
of cardboard into rectangular boxes,
one piece a lid, the other a base,
a bit of folding, positioning
the edges so they lined up,
then pressing the foot pedal,
three staples thump thump thump
into each corner, the lid and base
connected, the two halves
pieced together, then stacked
one upon the other below
the wire mesh windows.

Each afternoon after school
box after box slid into a neat stack,
several sizes, one for each
coat brought down on the rack
from upstairs. Sewing machines
drilled cloth to cloth, shoulder
to sleeve, button to breast,
from early morning to late evening.
The women over their machines
spoke little, clipped the thread,
tugged the seams, repositioned
for another run.
                     Each coat,
inspected and labeled by Martha,
swung down on a conveyor to shipping
like minimum wage dancers, first
the car coats, then the waist jackets,
finally, the furs (collars
attached by metal hooks), gentled
with the palm, laid in white tissue.

Alley Window

Above
the spots of oil,
the glitter
of bottle glass,
paint peels
on the sill, the
sash glazing
curled up
like ribs,
wavy glass
dark as a
dog's eye.
There is
little indication
the window
has ever
been opened.

Yet, surely
before air
conditioning,
a man
in a vest,
a woman
in a waistcoat,
leaned out
into the alley
with lit
cigarettes, elbows
bent, hands
loosened at
the wrists,
considering
the hours
left on the

clock, the red
brick framing
their faces,
damp collars
cooling in
the small
breeze.

a six cent Green River

Dogs Have Changed

and I blame it on World War II.
My kids treat their dogs like children,
taking them to sitters or doggie hotels
when they're out of town. They hire a girl
to walk them and to pick up their shit
in plastic bags. They even have health insurance
that will pay the vet for routine visits,
teeth cleaning, ass gland expunging. It's odd
how different dogs have become. As a boy,
I loved my pets, all of them, about one per year.
In my day (as the old are prone
to say), we didn't fence our dogs. They ran
wild from dawn to dark. They romped
and sniffed, drank muddy water, ate
dead animals, and chased semi-trucks
down by the highway. Some were fast.
Dad gave me his Army entrenching tool.
He told me to keep it folded,
within easy reach
for the next shellacking.

The Antique Cheeseburger

John the Baptist lived on locusts
and honey, not my choice,
but I'm certain he could slide into 32
waist Levi's. Jesus attended a number
of well-larded meals. The New Testament
speaks of them. Little is said though
of any weight gain, or weight loss.
After 40 days and nights in the desert,
did he imagine a cheeseburger and fries
when he stepped on the bathroom scale
and peered between his dusty toes
at the numbers? Likewise, I doubt
that he ordered the Caesar salad
at the last supper. Someone
should do a study of ancient diet plans,
Romans on the Atkinson, gluten-free Mongols,
a step-watch for Greeks at Marathon.

Stand-Up Cat

I find myself telling jokes
to my cat, but he's so easily distracted
by odd shifts of shadow and light
that he rarely pays attention to
my punch line. He sees what I don't.
Possibly, ghosts, dimensions foreign
to me. He moans and whines
at invisible stirrings, flies
up the stairs, climbs curtains,
arches his spine, snickers
at my slowness to catch on.
If I could see ghosts, a poltergeist, a spirit,
then I wouldn't be so reliant on irony
or deadpan. I'd be vaudevillian,
a foot in the bucket. Really, it's true.
I'd throw a tomato back at the hecklers,
a cabbage, a plum. I'd walk out
under a streetlight
where the cats are giggling
over small bags of catnip,
where one old Tom on a fence rail
wails in stand-up cat lingo,
Hey, I'm dying up here.

Owner's Manual

When the children's dogs are visiting, it is difficult for our cat. He's the rightful owner of the beanbag chair in the basement. Maybe that's why the dogs want to kill him. They think he stinks of entitlement. The cat has a chair. He has two bowls. One for dry food, one for canned. He drinks out of the toilet. The dogs chase him around the house when he dashes from bed to bathroom. I tell my wife that this isn't a good situation. If the dogs catch him, he'll lacerate their noses with his claws. That's why I've started carrying him around the house. She says, he's not disabled. I tell her, just kick him out for a few days. He'll do well outside where there's hundreds of dogs he can disfigure. It's too hot, she says. He'll dehydrate. Set a bowl of water out for him, I reply. You know he hates bowls, she answers. I didn't know. Later that day, I notice the plumber is in the backyard installing a toilet on the deck. What the hell? I ask. The plumber is an old friend of the family. He knows more about us than our marriage counselor. He hands me the American Standard owner's manual. Make sure you turn the water off and drain the tank this winter, or the cat's got a problem.

Polio Turtle

It took ten cents to ride the bus uptown,
and then a penny to give the elevator boy
(although he was a man) to take us to the fourth
floor of the Professional Building. The doctor
charged $5 a visit, but he let mom pay it out
over time. She said that with five kids
the doctor's account was revolving. Afterwards,
we walked to Chubb's where she bought
me a six cent Green River in a paper cone.
Not counting the doctor's bill, Mom and I could spend
the day for 17 cents each. Lunch at Woolworth's
was out of the question, so was the Five and Dime
unless I needed a shot or stitches. Then I could
choose from anything under 49 cents.
Polio closed the city pool that summer, and
the following fall the school kids
were fed sugar cubes. I wondered
what an iron lung would earn me at Kress's toy counter.
When my best friend got sick,
mom broke down and bought me a painted turtle.
He crawled on colored pebbles
below a plastic palm tree.

Tying Flies

Rain froze on the driveway
late this afternoon. I'd come home
early for my four o'clock nap.
The trash containers were still
on the curb so I thought I should
pull them up into the garage.
I slipped on the new ice
but only briefly since it was
patchy, the cold not having
gotten to it all. There was mail
in the mailbox, all bills or junk
advertisements. I wadded them
into my coat pocket and started
up the slippery slope to the house.
My wife was already home, busy
with something. Can't recall what.
The tree beside the house, an ornamental
of some type, was scraping the paint
in the steady wind, fingers
clicking against the wallboard.
I thought of my brother, back
when he was smaller than me,
hunched over his desk, squinting
at the flies he was tying. Neither
of us ever fished for anything more
than perch. I hadn't remembered
the bottle-blues in years, the
small red feathers, or the hook eyes.
I guess it was my brother's long fingers,
his small rounded shoulders,
practicing, as I teased, for old age,
the rain turning in the cold
to the ice we fear today.

Jell-O kingpins

Billy Collins Pisses Me Off

Not because he has snubbed me
at a social gathering,
or stumbled over the pronunciation
of my name because that hasn't

happened. I think he's cosmopolitan
enough to handle Italian surnames.
It's more like he takes every
good idea that I should have thought

and plays it perfectly into a poem
that I haven't written. No kidding,
I read him every morning,
and inevitably, I think. Damn.

That's the poem I should have written.
It's like we are fishing for trout
in some Colorado stream,
and although we plop our flies

only feet apart, he keeps pulling
out the fish. This happened
to me once at Red Feather Lake.
This lady, who wasn't Billy Collins,

even loaned me her kernels of yellow corn,
and we dropped line after line
into a deep hole behind
a partially submerged rock. Finally,

out of kindness I suppose, she
gave me half her stringer
of lake trout, and my entire family
ate like effing kings.

Caught Naked with Her

As a young janitor, working
my way through college, I
stumbled into a painting studio

where a woman I'd known
from the Work/Study Program
posed nude, a black scarf

trailing one thigh. (Easily,
the only memorable moment
in my janitorial career.) Yet,

when our eyes met, I felt
embarrassed for sweeping so well,
for using the dustpan, the little

whisk, for seeing her naked
with a broom in my hand.
In hindsight which is 20/20

I should have excused myself,
backed out with my rubber
trash barrel banging the doorjamb.

Visiting the Retina Specialist

I sit in the waiting room
with a bus load of old women
in stocking caps, a few having
scooted in with walkers.
They are a pleasant bunch,
shuttled from the assisted living.
Together, we watch an early morning
television program on decoupage.
Young couples are teamed up
to scout an outdoor flea market,
haggling over weathered furniture.
They buy what they can
on a limited budget. They commend
one another on having a good eye.
Upon returning to their workshops,
they glue old maps, photographs,
fabric to the tops of tables and stools.
One couple takes a perfectly good
set of ice cream chairs and welds them
into a bench which is actually
too small to sit in comfortably.
Eventually, they are the winners,
having turned the greater profit
at a consignment auction.
I quit watching when another team
in a subsequent episode
glues a set of books together,
drills a hole through them,
slides in a burnished metal pipe,
and creates a lamp for better reading.
I return to my collected poems
of WS Merwin, and try to make sense
of line after line without
punctuation marks.
Seeing is difficult as it is.
Soon, I will be gluing his poems
on a small step ladder. It can
be used in a library with high shelves.

Pharmacy Run

They find each other waiting in lines
for prescription refills and begin to speak
of ailments. Nothing clicks like
it once did. There are no flashing lights
or musical accompaniments.
They realize that more time is needed,
more time for the moments
that slipped away. Always the lights are low.
More creams are involved, more pills.
Still they fumble for one another,
undressing with their backs turned,
stepping first out of their shoes, creasing
shirts and pants over a chair, pausing
with the curtains drawn.

Morning Feathers

When I step out onto the porch, a V of wild geese
honk southward away from the coming winter.

The clouds reflect the lights of 87th Street,
incandescent, bright with city ambience.

I have stored boxes of journals, poems, rough drafts
of novels. I keep them for a rainy afternoon

with my grandchildren. Today, it's time for them
to find arrowheads, pottery, owl feathers.

In this drought I take them to the Kaw River
where we walk emerging sandbars with a leaf rake,

scratching the river-smoothed surface
for what's been buried or dropped in flight.

Guilt Trip

In every phone call
with my mother
there comes a point
when dialogue
narrows to monologue,
and she insists
that she'd be
better off dead
than at the assisted living.
Usually, I
change the subject
to some cheerful
antic of a grandchild.
Lately, she's begun
reminding me
that she never sees
her grandchildren,
that they couldn't
pick her out
of a line-up.

She shuffles in
with other grandmothers
below a height chart,
under a glaring
white bulb, all
assisted living
escapees, wheelchair
hijackers, Jell-O kingpins.
My three-year-old
waves to her
behind the see-through
mirror, but grandmother
is stuck on the other side
of her reflection.
CNAs lead her away
with Adeline
and Bertie and Opal.

Alf Chooses the Cherry Pie

The old man at assisted living
sits among his family this Sunday.
They whirl around him like leaves.
He sits mostly with his hands on his lap,
considering the menu for today's meal
like he might a hymn in Latin.
His grandson, a young man now,
calls him Poppy, congratulates him
on his choice of pie. Again,
the old man looks bewildered, stares
into the incandescence. He is the
elephant in the room. The family
directs the side dishes to his plate,
the potatoes, the greens, the soft rolls.

Alf Considers the Next Big Thing

The average expectancy is what
for the American male, 76.4 years?
It keeps changing, you know,
the time remaining. And one day
when you tally up the motorcycle,
the sports car, the goatee, the Stevie
Nicks hall pass, you finally admit
your AARP card is not a fake ID
for senior discounts at motels, cinema
tickets, bungee jumps, excursions
to Precious Moments, any place where
you don't have to walk much
or show your bony knees.

Alf Works the South Hallway

Two sparrows landed on my windowsill
and waved their little wing tips at me.
And I thought, yea, big deal, so you
want a love letter. Why not one written
by a woman in a Walmart housecoat
about how irresistible I am? There's
plenty of paper and stubby pencils
at the assisted living, but the words
the old girls write are menu selections
for the evening meal. I'm thinking
how about later when the orderlies
are playing cards, and the hall lights
are dimmed like a June evening.
Depends? Yea, I got Depends.

We Were English Majors Once

The bar is empty when I walk in
so, I take a pint glass
and draw my own from the tap.
The back door opens, and Liz,
along with three regulars
trail in from their smoke break.
I offer her money for the beer
and order a Jack Daniels neat.

She says, hey, try this new one,
and with a little slight-of-hand,
she sets up a Diet Coke instead.
At first, I'm thinking, ok, what gives?
But then she laughs, and I realize
she's messing with me,
so, I lean over the bar
in pretend revenge, and I swear
to god on accident, my hand
falls like a caress
across the front of her sweater.
It's a tender too much, too late.

Today, there's a rhythm to us,
less poetry, more chopped prose.
We've read it all before anyway.
She wipes a ring clean with the bar rag,
and slips a coaster under my glass.

Watching the Solar Eclipse in the Rain

We cheer each parting of the clouds,
the sun a clipped Roman coin,
growing smaller, yet more
significant by the minute. Eclipse
Totality is partly obscured,
the diamond ring, the black sun
swallowed behind low clouds.

Rain spatters our cheap paper glasses.
A boy in a lawn chair cries
that he will miss it, miss it all.
I say a little prayer that the clouds
will part, a gift for those who
have traveled far. Even the high school band
has tuned up, ready to burst
with brass and drum.

                Laughing,
my daughters dance, twirling their arms
in quixotic windmills, blowing
the clouds, pushing them away
from the darkening sun. Their children
stand ready for what may be
a once in a lifetime experience
with cans of silly string,
glow sticks decorating their necks
like ancient amulets.

My Brother and I Break Dance at Another Family Wedding

It's expected of us, even as sixty-year-olds. Our sisters, cousins, nieces, nephews circle round the center of the dance floor, and leave us to clown with satirical skills. One of these days, I told an older friend, my heart pounding from our silly spinning, I won't get up. He nods his head in thought. Yes, but that wouldn't be so bad, he adds. And taken by the thought, I agree. Carted off the dance floor on a gurney would provide years of family anecdotes. He died doing what he loved they'd say, which isn't exactly the case, but close enough. Crowds, dance floors, rock & roll, are part of my past. Now, I'm more concerned with oxygen, and the quiet over a cup of coffee. Still, as dying goes, there's much which is good in a break dance collapse, the laughter of the family pounding in my ears, the dizziness when I try to stand, reaching for my wife who understands I exaggerate my wobble to cover the real weakness, the spinning white table cloths, the cake, the kegs of cheap beer. I should write an apology to the bride du jour and keep it pinned in the breast pocket of my wedding suit. I'm sorry for dying at your wedding reception. Feel free not to include the EMTs, their red bags, blue cargo pants, the yellow defibrillator among your wedding pictures, unless somehow the colors coordinate with the bride maids' dresses, the sprays of baby breath, the icing on the cake.

up to his knuckles in Kimchee

Abbey Raises Chickens

The neighborhood cats
have never faced off
against a peck-ready,
sharp-spurred farm cock.
Suburban cats are champions
of sidewalks and patios,
hunters of chipmunks
and slow sparrows.
One morning, my niece,
a suburban transplant
to cock and hen farming,
took off running in her
Nikes, the county road
a ribbon stretched
to the next section, only
to find a red-combed
rooster chasing her
step by step. He flapped
his wings, squawked,
and kicked his spurs.
Her heels punched
the August dust
like .22 slugs. Whitman,
her literary, sit-on-the-
book-and-preen cat,
slipped from the barn,
and dashed bat shit crazy
through a hole
in the backdoor screen.

General Tso's Chicken

The Chinese delivery man
greets me on my porch
with a plastic bag of pork
fried rice and General Tso's
chicken. I sign my debit slip
and hand him five bucks
as a tip. The wind whirls.

Leaves rattle across the pavement—
lizard feet, cat claws,
gravel scattered with
a baseball bat. The
pinon pine from a neighbor's
chimney disguises the air
with romance, but mostly, it is
a night to close the door—

Netflix, Hulu, Amazon
below the winter clouds.
Chef Peng, photographed
with Henry Kissinger,
popularized the General's
Chicken. Peng
in fleeing Chairman Mao
opened restaurants in Taiwan
and later New York, saving

Tso's recipe from communism.
(It is easy to know this
with Google.) Chen retreats
to his car. We wave briefly.

The night is blustery, edged
with chill, as old as the wind
that blows under doors.

Chickens Are Still Chickens

This young lady comes into the
hostel commons with soft-boiled eggs,
mashed up to resemble scrambled,
piled on buttered toast. During the night,
after some hard drinking, she'd booked
a flight on Travelocity for Bali.
(Sometimes she surprises herself
more than she does her mother.)
She laughs it off with her girlfriend
between gulps of coffee, brushing
her hair out of her eyes with a calm
flip of her fingers. The eggs and toast
will see her through today.
No doubt, she'll find more
half-way to India, another hemisphere
where chickens are still chickens,
eggs scrambled,
or over-easy in a pocket of toast.

In Search of Quivira We Found Chicken Fried Rice

Coronado chose the shrimp.
He was always picking
the most expensive item
on the menus. He was
like that, his penchant for
more than he had—ate him
the way he ate the shrimp,
dipping it furiously
up to his knuckles in Kimchee.
There's nothing wrong with
wanting. It's human I suppose.
But sometimes you
climb a high butte, a tree,
a tall step ladder, and take
a look at where you are,
the Great American Desert,
as maps labeled it, stretching
from Texas through Kansas
to Canada, to the Arctic. No spires
of gold. Just MasterCard, VISA,
Discover. Chicken fried rice.
I should say something to him.

Peeing at McDonald's after Eating a Chicken Sandwich

A half a dozen men like me
sit at separate tables.
Each is hunched
over a chicken sandwich
and fries, #5, the cashier
calls it. We look a lot alike,
these old men and I,
graying in mutually exclusive
circles, swivel chairs pointed
so as not to be in direct line
with the swivel of another.
When I rest my book by my tray
and step into the bathroom,
an old man in a hoodie
labors over the urinal
tugging at his zipper.
Men avoid looking at each other
at urinals. We set our eyes
on the ceiling, the tile wall,
our dicks. We trust anonymity.
It is work enough to open the valves
in privacy, to pretend
they close upon command,
the spotless porcelain,
like my father used to say,
as clean as a whistle.

Suffering on the Floor of a Fast Food Bathroom Stall I Imagine Amerigo Vespucci in Japan

There's a pattern to my stupidity,
one where I drift along in a pretty
normal day to day routine,

and then for no apparent reason,
I end up on the floor of a toilet stall
in gut-wrenching pain, trying to

negotiate a method to puke
and shit my brains out at the same time.
I know what you're thinking

that I'd gone on a drinking binge
and was now paying for it in a john
without toilet paper (which I didn't

realize until too late). But my illusions,
if you will, aren't facilitated by alcohol.
I'm pretty much free range in grandeur.

I took the Dante's Inferno Challenge
at a sushi bar, for which I was awarded
a white t-shirt, printed up like the
release form I signed, guaranteeing

the owners that I would not sue them
if I ended up like I ended up.
It was a spontaneous moment,

but I was certain I could put to shame
a full ghost pepper sushi roll
in five minutes without recourse

to water, or milk, or beer, or crackers,
or bland white rice, while the sushi chefs
and waitress and manager and a few
customers took photos. I think

what confused me was the mix
of the Italian literary allusion
and the haiku of a little fish
wrapped in seaweed.

I felt like an early Italian explorer
sailing into Yokohama or Osaka,
wooden keel cutting towards paper houses,
and then at anchor, bartering terza rima

for puffer fish. But I was mistaken.
The Portuguese sailed to Japan first,
not the Italians, and certainly,
not Amerigo Vespucci.

Biscuit Boy

The cashier went missing
right in the middle of my burrito
order. The manager to mollify
the line at the window
comped us our drinks. I guess
that meant we didn't have to pay.
A boy from the back,
probably more skilled in biscuits,
toyed with the register.
My breakfast burrito with the comped
orange juice came up on the screen
at $345.95. He scratched the part
of his head that stood up
behind his visor, a curly patch
of unruly dishwater. He apologized
for the inconvenience and comped me
for curly fries, which were not
even a part of the burrito breakfast.
After a time, the manager
returned with the cashier, who
had obviously been crying, likely
in the walk-in because her hands
were blue and splotchy.
She cleared the register and re-entered
my order. The orange juice
no longer comped, the curly fries
reconfigured to hash browns.

Drinking with the Governor

This is not the time for me
to tell him what I think of his
tax cuts that stripped public
school funding, or his
dissolution of the State's art
commission. There's a wheel
among wheels for that. This is a
reception for novelists, memoirists,
and poets. So, he probably has
an inclination of where we stand.
He drinks white wine, greets guests
at the door of the mansion, polite
as a fisherman in a small boat.
I drink locally brewed beer, eat
catered finger food. The ice chest
on the veranda appears bottomless.
Chargers of shrimp appear
like compromises.

By accident, we bump into
each other in the house library.
He shows the Jameson boy a secret
panel in the wall. If you push it
in just the right spot, a door opens
and there's an antique safe inside
for which someone at some time
held the combination. Jameson
puts his ear to the steel and turns
the dial. The room quiets
like maybe he can really hear
tumblers clicking into place.

Nearly Poor White People

It doesn't take long before
you notice that flea markets
across America have about
the same of everything
lining their shelves:
chipped head vases, sad irons, the
ubiquitous sausage grinder.
Even still, there's usually
a vendor that you frequent.
You keep hoping that
one day, probably a Monday
or Tuesday, after the weekend
garage sales, you'll
find that one piece of pink depression
that you've been looking for.
On Saturday mornings
mothers drag their children
along with them. The kids
are impatient, want
McDonald's Happy Meals,
cheap toys. Their mothers
tow them with promises
of hamburgers, chicken strips,
a better life.

eats rarely, sinks like a rock

The Used Bookstore Buys More than a Papercut

You were listening to NPR's *All Things Considered*
just as you do every day. There was coffee.
A woman with red hair walked in. She sold
you a signed copy of *Howl*. She explained
that a friend had given it to her. She'd wanted him
as a lover. But all she got was this book

which doesn't make much sense, now
that she's emptying her shelves,
coloring ducks with her grandchildren.
She remembers the poet reading it in Lawrence,
back in the 80s, but even then,
it was dimming for her
like a bright bulb behind a dusty shade.

Whitman as Coyote

The stars on this night of scattered clouds
remind me how small I am, compared to the
timeless chill, the faraway, uncaring
loneliness. There is little which is more
lasting in a star than longing, the call
to discover what is missing, unthought
or bound by popular constraint.
In this sense, stars are unrealized dreams
tossed from coyote's blanket, too far
away to touch, too close, yet, not to try.
The old poet, walking into the yard, sensed
within the Milky Way an order too broad
for NASA, for space stations, for astronauts,
teasing them, emptiness be damned.

The Potted Sonnet

If I sit behind the rolltop desk, even
with the sunlit window, I need one bulb
snapped on. Through the shade, the light
is as green as a houseplant. The shadows
as dark as potting soil. There is a white planter
where I've nursed a philodendron

for over 40 years. Cuttings hang in pots
in a dozen corners. If these vines
keep growing, they'll reconnect as if
across a rainforest floor, circles within circles,
rooting for purchase. At some point
in the dim light, the growth slows, bends

to a withered end. Either, the metaphor
dies, or nothing rhymes with orange.

A Life Jacket for Oliver

Two moments standout in my mind, Churchill's
Iron Curtain speech and my daughter's discovery
of a jack-in-the-pulpit on yesterday's hike, an odd
mix, wildflowers, and speeches by Englishmen.
Both were photo ops, moments that compelled me
to step back and reconsider rural Missouri.
Oliver, the old Shi-Tzu, nearly blind, mostly
deaf, wakes each morning only to find
another place to sleep.
                                        He gives me pause
when I consider the final years. He hasn't
barked in months, eats rarely, sinks like a rock
in the lake, so we wrap him in a life jacket,
in case he should take a rare, wrong step,
and float belly-up into a photograph.

Wild Geese

I always follow the flight of geese
when they're just above the treetops,
pumping their wings, forming their echelon.
Who doesn't look up? Maybe
those of us who are most distracted,
absorbed by purpose, like some poor guy
with a shirt and tie, wrangling his keys,
probably a meeting in mind, a weight
bearing down on his shoulders. Once,
in New York City, a man passed on the sidewalk
with a cat sitting on his head. The cat, a weight,
was his Village stich. They walked easily,
a man with a turban, a cat with a view.
                              That was that.

The Argument

She rakes leaves
from the flower beds
and I churn them up
with the mower, always
one side of the house
between us, our silence
like a coming rain. The faster
I mow and dump
the churned mulch
into bio-degradable paper,
the quicker she pulls yesterday
into the yard. If we actually
fought, threw down the words
that hurt, little would
get done around here.
We wait for a clean lawn
before garaging the tools.
Yesterday's winds
stuffed in bags, not forgotten,
but lined along the curb
for the landfill.

Xanax and coffee latte

Bad Eye

The truth to what I see
is blurred, no matter
how I turn my head or tilt
my glasses on my nose.
One eye still works for
reading, for scribbling
notes on a page. This
morning I sprained my
ankle, stepping down
a stair that wasn't a stair.
The pain has spread
to an ache in my soul.
My mother went like this,
vision blurred by stroke,
body bending to the north
from something relentless
like the constant Kansas
wind of it. In the end
she walked with a tilt,
stepping from curbs
that weren't curbs, into
streets that weren't streets.
Now I understand
her grip on my arm,
how her one good eye
only saw how badly
the bad eye failed.

slicing the five o'clock cake

retirement party/red fruit punch
mixed with seven-up/plates
of oatmeal cookies/choice
of raisins/chocolate chips/a
party-mix sea-salted *(no one
really wants to be here)*
it's not personal/you've waited
at the punch bowl time and again/
just one more stop before
the parking lot/the social committee
passes a card/a black ink pen *(say
something more than good-bye)*
but that's all it is/a series of bites/
forks in icing/hey champ/
enjoy the fishing/the grandchildren/
volunteer at church carnivals/
golf/fish/golf/fish/
collect blankets/warm the homeless/
this is the last big thing before
the last big thing/white cake served
on a cardboard platter

cleaning the inbox

ran through my email, a bit
backlogged since i've been away,
much i simply delete, sharply
hitting the correct keys, like
cleaning the kitchen after
several days of stacking dishes,
only this is much easier, emptying
the inbox takes a quick click,
and since i've added the sound app,
i can hear the clutter, swished
into cyber-oblivion, it's a good
feeling, a cleanliness of sorts,
which may in some ways,
be closer to godliness than
i realize, since here and now,
with the inbox empty, i'm
open to the next wave, some
i subscribe too, certainly, the insights
from the buddhist center,
mindfulness, loving kindness, etc.,
quite christian i think,
especially during the Merry season, then
facebook, some group or another
i've shouldered up with,
a favorite from the guy
with the metal detector who posts
pictures of dug-up dimes, crucifixes,
dog tags, reminders
tarnished, worn
like a fingerprint, which may
in themselves

trigger something akin
to the spiritual, and if not, well,
i can click delete
more easily than hauling out
the chicken bones, pizza boxes,
crematorium advertisements

First Walk in the Rain after Retirement

I walk in a slow drizzle
through the catalpa grove,
retired finally, at home
with time. There's
a metal bridge
with wooden planks
that rattle under each step,
a humming bee tree, a black
snake below a log,
the soil as dark and fertile
as the next big thing.

Dust Jacket

I have a box of used books,
several boxes in fact. They've
been abandoned, thumbed
through, a few chapters read

in this one, a dozen poems
in another. Now, I have
these pages that fell short
of my expectations.

Throwing them out with
the plastic bags from yesterday's
kitchen slop is not an option.
Even failed promises are worthy
of some respect. So, I load them
into the trunk of the car
and drive to Half-Price Books
where a clerk removes them

from the banana box. Even
with a clean dust jacket,
a few cents on the dollar
is the best we can expect.

Interrupting the Artist

As
  the phone
    began to ring
      I wondered
        how many times
          it would take
            for a man of 90
              to walk from
                his studio
                  to silence
                    the jingling

      rotary-dial.
      Only one
      telephone
     in a house
    so large, for a man
    so small,
   would he even
   bother to pick up,
    knowing the
     light lost
      in an afternoon
       is gone
        forever?
         The interruption of

    a brushstroke
    means more
    today
     than whatever a
     Meals on Wheels
       tomorrow
         holds.

Walking under September Pines

It's the scent of them mostly
that strikes me in the bone-deep heat,
the sun beating white across the streets,
the wind nearly indistinguishable
from my slow thoughts. A single bee
drones heavily. Yet, there is within
the branches a movement, more
of a nudge towards autumn
than a passage between seasons.
I walk on a sidewalk
littered with needles, browned
like the thousand moments
that have fallen. A yellow flower
bends at the edge of change.

Good Friday

The rain began as I left the house,
a calming drizzle
like a Xanax and coffee latte.
Now, at work, a newscast bleeds
through an adjoining wall.

Nothing intelligible, only the crackle
of my inner Syria, temporarily,
a distant thunder. The rain falls,
drums the window, soothes
my need to engage. It returns
throughout the morning
as a mantra in lamb's blood,
as a Jewish woman filling
her palms with myrrh.

Sleeping in Railroad Cave

We woke in the darkness, looking out
into the light, the entrance curtained
with ice. The sunlight caught
as it would behind a window,
luminescent like the first sun.
Already, trickles of melt were running
in barely detectable currents, cold beads
on the tips of the frozen. By midmorning,
the ice would drop, a harvest loosened
from the limestone. Reluctantly,
we kicked our way out. The span of ice
shattered with the force of our boots
across the leaf fall. We emerged
into the early sun, cold pinching our nostrils,
each step a snapping twig, a circling crow,
a woodpecker drumming wood.

The Calico Mayor

Here in the rain with the tornado sirens blaring
I find myself in a parking lot with a bar on one side
and a funeral home on the other. Somewhere
in between, Siri says there's a poetry reading
at a popular coffee shop. Siri has messed with me
before, once in Ireland, she sent me down
a one lane road into an oncoming combine.
There was no room to turn around, so I backed up
nearly to Dingle. And all the while the crone
keeps saying *continue continue.* Tonight ushers
more urgency with the storm lifting trees out of
root sockets. I have an audience waiting,
even if they have taken shelter in a warehouse
basement. I'd join them if I could, read a poem
about sunlight or a village of stray Irish cats,
the calico mayor bristling a WTF outside a famine hut,
my fender crumpled against a quaint stonewall.

Flying Over the Coast of Greenland

The boy in the next seat moves
his laptop so I can join him
at the window. At 30,000 feet
the shoreline appears unapproachable,
jagged Vs, consonants of ocean and crag.
At night would a village light be visible,
a slip for a boat, a minnow
of beach? Even at this height,
there are no soft lines.
Only after time and distance
do we begin to see—contour
blending into contour. How high
will the pilot have to take us
before Greenland's coast smooths?
The boy flies alone from Dublin.
Between parents, he plays video games,
examines glacier fjords
with a stranger from Kansas.

Moving the Elks Club Piano

Five men captured in a photograph
roll an upright piano across
the main street in town. It is a
country town in the lowlands
of southern Kansas. A few cars
have slowed to a stop at the traffic light.
One woman is leaning from her window
with a broad sunshine-filled smile.
A man in a truck has his hand
up to his chin. He appears concerned.
Maybe he has moved a piano before
and is already considering the coming
jump up the curb. The trick is in
keeping the piano upright, one man
with his hands high on the sound board,
two, maybe three lifting, the last
of them in back with his shoulder
placed high, one foot wedged
to keep it from rolling back
into the street like a memory.

At the Home for Imbecilic Youth

A few crows caw along the fence line, scavenge the roadside for refuse, for litter, for cast off Happy Meals. There's little chance of a selfie in this rain, the façade I want to capture too far in the distance for affect. The 19th century name drew me the way the crows are drawn to trash.

I wanted to capture a bit of antiquated language, caustic, appealing in its lack of modern political correctness. Later, the name would change to The Home for the Feeble Minded. I suppose to tone a more equitable sentiment. Possibly, to open the doors to a wider clientele. In time the doors were shut, allegations of abuse, chains, shackles, locks without keys found in basement storage. Sometimes, when I consider whether mankind has evolved into a more civilized version of itself, I remember this stonework, the way it stood behind the landscape of my face, a castle of sockets, darkening in the April rain. The crows still feed on the roadside, some I imagine land on the windowsills, peck the eyeballs from the glass.

Green Tara

I know a woman who lives in a cave. It's not a muddy Ozark cave with a small creek and brown bats building guano piles. No, it's more like a room chiseled out of the face of a mountainside. I've seen a picture. She's sitting at a painted table with a tea pot on a small stove. There's a wall-hanging like a mandala behind her, a few books, a vase. The cave has seen a woman's touch and has been swept clean, softened by textile, by textures unknown to rock. There's no running water or electricity, like I said, it's a cave in a mountain, not an apartment below a bar jokingly dubbed "the cave." I'd like to throw my sleeping bag down on the floor and watch the sun rise through the door. There's little more I can say. Her experiences are so different than mine. Probably, she's ridden a motorcycle, fast like the wind itself. Probably, she's been hurt in love. Probably, she's danced until the what-ifs and what-the-fucks poured out of her skin. Probably, she chose a cave because it was dependable, like hope, not because she had piles of throw pillows that needed a home.

a small goat smothered in salsa

Goats Unbidden

During the morning, before
we had completely opened our eyes,
a small herd of goats bleated
through the abandoned building
where we'd been trying to sleep.
A rooster had flown into some kind
of Mexican tree before the sun rose
and had begun crowing. My girlfriend
threw her hairbrush into the branches.
That was before the goats arrived,
and before we'd added a cheerful
aspect to our faces. The goats,
on the other hand,
were much more polite
than the rooster. A man
and two dogs accompanied them.
We *como se llama'd* and then
como se dice'd and shared
a cigarette. The dogs, as non-smokers,
drove the goats down the valley
to a bright spot where the early sun
shimmered like water.
These were hard times in Mexico.
A bottle of beer cost 3500 pesos.
Local mechanics took their spare change
and drilled them into washers;
juveniles broke open Fresca machines
and stole slugs. At the only café
in town, we shared
a small goat smothered in salsa.
I do not speak Spanish. I thought
I had ordered the fish.

Ashes

After my father died, my mother
spent her days sorting through
his closets, giving away armloads
of clothes, unused tools, electric gadgets,
especially watches, purchased
from the shopping channel
for 19.95 or less. It was his way
of saying America to the poverty
of the immigrant, the Valley of Ashes
only miles from his door.
Cleaning out my own house years later,
I move boxes of books, notebooks of old
poems, spirals of unfinished novels,
all that my father and mother
gave me, the shirt on my back,
graduate school, sheaves of
college ruled paper. You can be
anything you want they said.

Creeping South

Late at night when most have
taken to their beds, he coasts eighth street
on the slowest bicycle in town. Without
central air, the doors and windows
are open for whatever breeze
is free. He recognizes some,
sweating in lumpy chairs, following
the blue roll of *The Tonight Show*,
others are little more than a shadow,
a cigarette rising at midnight.
He knows who cannot sleep,
who waits for a lifting wind,
a thunderstorm, a police siren, a bottle
breaking on a curb. In the shotgun house
on the corner, a woman steps to her
front door in nothing but a man's shirt.
She cups her hands to her face
and looks into the street. He circles
the block back to her house,
but the door is now closed. The window lit
by a lamp with a faded yellow shade.

Taking the Chipmunk Seriously

The cat plays with small animals
in the backyard. He toys with them
until they no longer move, then bored,
he retreats to a patch of sun on the porch.
Today, our daughter slides open the glass door,
scolding the cat into submission.
A chipmunk flees below the redwood deck
where another dozen huddle in the darkness.
They embrace his journey, his odyssey,
his rescue by the child goddess
with the bare feet, toenails painted
with blood. A chant issues from their throats
like the wind. They lift their paws
to fecundity. Tonight, they dance.

Cow Creek Snow

I remember you running
through the curtain
that was the door to your
bedroom, and retrieving
a hatchet from under
your bed, just a fragment
of a memory, boys
with important plans
that required a small axe
to cull a clearing
along Cow Creek, sharpening
stakes into lances
for a redoubt.

I sent flowers to the funeral home
after a Facebook post, having read
that you were a grandfather,
retired from a lifetime
of sharpening stakes, from
tearing down and rebuilding
in a town we'd never considered
as boys. Along Cow Creek
in the dense vine-hung woods,
we found a fox skin in the snow,
you peeled it from the bone
with the hatchet's edge, the fox's
red tail soft, windswept
in the winter sun.

Goldfinch Burial

We found three goldfinches
below the Rose of Sharon,
stuffed toys within three feet
of each other. One was still alive,
so, the kids put him in a shoebox,
lined with soft green grass,
and placed him in the small branches
away from the cat. He rode
out the rest of his life
buoyed by their hope of flight.
I buried him with the other two
in the corner of the garden
below the Japanese maple.
My granddaughter asked
if I knew where I was digging.
You've buried a lot there, she said,
squirrels, rabbits, chipmunks, cats.
You might find old bones.
The curve of my foot fit
the shovel's blade. I pushed,
splitting the black soil,
worm rich, digging deeply
for better forgetting.

Before It's Too Late

So, I'm driving down the highway
with Death in the backseat, and he's
chewing my ear off like he's prone,
when this crotch rocket of a Kawasaki
goes flying by on the inside shoulder,
and then back into traffic, weaving
between two semis and then on
towards the head of the snake, and Death
laughs out loud, *I just love that guy.*
Young, dumb, and full of cum.
I'm so fed up with his cliché crap
that I decide to tell him before it's too late,
You know, you're a dick.
Death winks at me in the rearview mirror.
That's what she said.

Memorial Day Weekend

This morning I rise late
to find my wife
cleaning the cabinets.
The chairs are pushed against
the wall. She has already
mopped the floors with her
new Wet Mop Swifter.
The coffee is made.
I drag one chair to the small
kitchen table and write
a poem about her.
I keep it in my pocket
like a buckeye, like
a match, like an old letter
saved for decades.

Writing a Love Poem while the Plumber Snakes the Basement Drain

I wonder what he'll dredge up,
Tampons, tree roots, Kleenex,
bits of a dog toy. We've had
work done before. It's kept us
going through the years, the old
house in constant need of attention.
Once, all that was mundane
we hungered for, even now,
at the kitchen table, the snake
churning through the main drain,
the who-knows-what
we've flushed, the messiness
behind years of stacked boxes,
labeled in permanent marker.

Cabin in the Woods

Here comes that old fantasy.
I can feel it emerging out of the quiet
of the rain-filled morning. You know,
the morning of peace, where the doves

coo from invisible branches
in the invisible trees. It's that special
fantasy of the cabin in the woods
with the screened windows open

to the summer air. And there's a table
in a single room with a small light
that is enough in itself to see
all that needs seen. And somewhere

in the faraway, a blue jay dips
a zig zagging line above pine needles.
Nothing is forever in this real place,
even the scent of leaves, turning

on the forest floor. Nothing carries
beyond the moment of light rain,
pattering the mailbox, dampening
the envelopes of bills and junk

advertisements. See how they curl,
sodden like an overused dream,
glue dissolving, sealed envelopes
opening themselves.

he nibbled at my gloved hand

Raising the Ladder

If I'd had an eye dropper, I would
have drawn it full of water
and dripped a few drops into
the bat's mouth. The pup, as ugly
as a comic book villain, had fallen
from the louvers below the cabin's
eave. I borrowed a ladder
and placed him above the reach
of raccoons and coyotes. He nibbled
at my gloved hand, the leather
a precaution against what I didn't
understand, some bat disease like
the ubiquitous rabies. Probably,
he didn't survive, curling
his pterodactyl wings into a shroud
against the drying wind. My grandchildren
assumed my prowess with ladders
was enough to raise life up
when it has fallen.

November Faces

There is a loneliness
in the singularity of falling
leaves at dusk,
the silhouettes of limbs,
the slant of rooftops,
the empty lawns. We turn
up the path towards home
to click all the electricity
we can into the lights.
Behind doors, we ladle
the warmth of supper
onto cold plates. We find
in the window's glass
our reflections, strangers
with familiar faces,
setting forks and spoons
in their places, always,
it seems, preparing.

High Ceilings

I like electric fans, especially
the old brass-bladed ones. Each
has its own peculiar sound,
a wobble, a bearing
slightly out of round. That said,
my favorite fan of all time
was fastened to the ceiling
in the old gym's training room.

My father as athletic trainer
had refashioned a crutch by
removing the rubber tip
and replacing it with white
tape and washers, a gapper
that he'd raise above his head
to switch the fan at its finial.
It would creak to a whir,
hum like a plane prop,
then the air would lift from
our shoulders, sweat drying,
cooling as if with a damp towel.

Coffee Tonight

A man with a beard on a snowy evening,
stands on the roadside beside his mailbox.
He looks about with expectation, up the road,
then down. He returns to his house empty-handed
and waits at the round table in the long dusk.
Sparrows settle in the wild roses; tomorrow
is a turn of the moon. As the day drains into night,
coyotes nose up from the creek bed, slipping
between strands of fence. When all is said,
coffee poured into a single cup, he crosses
a patch of window light, smoke in the air.

Weekenders

We have a small house
on a quiet cove on a busy
lake. Often, when we
step out onto the deck
after days of being absent,
we've seen a Great
Blue Heron, lifting
his wooden body with
ungainly wings into
the grove of trees along
Brush Creek. His nest
is near, fledglings,
a mate for the season.
The lake is artificial,
a frustration for the purist,
the naturalist, dammed
at the confluence of Ozark
rivers. For seventy years
the valley below has
been flooded, the thought
of it, now, murky, eerily
shifts in present tense.
The migration of pelicans,
hummingbirds, geese,
increases sales in binoculars,
water toys, Bud Light.
Weekenders in speed boats
lift cocktails
to the heron's flight, the
otherwise forgotten.

I Have Never Known a Hummingbird to Drink to Excess

Now, as the feeder sits on the deck rail
in want of a shepherd's hook,
it is only attracting large black ants,

the kind that startle us with bulbous bodies,
their commitment
to the colony, creepy and beautiful at once.

They gorge their way into the feeder,
a caravan drunk on sugary excess.
They float into the lurid red syrup,

a serendipitous drowning.
Most likely, the way all ants
dream of going, sucked up

into the maw of sweetness. Dreams
like a man might have, his excesses
taking him out of the world he knows,

his notion of all things in moderation
tossed aside like an average paperback.
So it is, he thinks to die in the arms

of a lover, their flesh a shroud.
How complete to end
deeper than ever before, a dying

more sea-struck than all the small
deaths combined, to flow
into another at last, and to surface

somewhere in their eyes
near the tear ducts, only
to be blinked out,

dabbed away with a tissue.
The ants in the bottle are flushed
with a hose, the deck washed clean

of sugar, the bottle refilled, hung high
for the hummingbirds who drink
only what flight can sustain.

after smashing peanuts

Cucumbers

You set your purse
on the doorstep of our
rental at Dickey Clay Pit,
and knelt before entering
to pull the weeds
from my cucumbers, the ones
I had ignored. You tossed
them in clumps by the door,
fast, heavy handfuls,
the brown earth
becoming visible again.

You were angry, not so much
at my laziness as a gardener,
but at the weeds,
their incessant return,
their reproach, and lack
of respect for ambition.
Even with your
gnarled hands, veined
and spotted with age,
your attack, personal,
verged on vendetta.
You cleared my patch
in minutes, and damned
if there weren't cucumbers
below, nearly a dozen,
as green and glossy
as what I'd imagined
when I stuck in the seeds.

Growing Tomatoes

is a lot like waiting
for Jesus. Each day

you pull up the lawn chair
next to your six leggy

plants. The yellow blossoms
and a few green

vegetables droop outside
the wire cages. You've tied

them with white rags,
a surrender bowed

to the soil. Dusted with
Sevin, they should be free

of aphids. You are not an
organic farmer. You are not

a farmer at all. You slice
tomatoes well, and that's

about it. You like them salted,
and spiced with chili peppers

between cold beers.
It is June. You have weeks to wait.

An asteroid could hit by
then. If you leave now,

you could be at a roadside
stand in Arkansas by sunset.

Surely, someone
is harvesting more than hope.

Two Truths about Fishing

A fisherman, swathed in a poncho,
trolls the water's edge. Morning rain
pocks the water, splatters
off the gunnels, the ballcap,
the fiberglass. The boat
moves quietly, barely creasing
the surface of the lake.
                        Overhead
the limbs of oaks, usually stretched
skyward, now, appear hooded,
bent like the fisherman who plumbs
the depths. Part of the truth he fishes
is as simple as a striking bass, the right
bait in the right spot.
                        The other truth,
is for quieter moments, that point
beyond the hook
which drops deeper still.

The Sleep of Emmett Kelly

There's a point after smashing peanuts
with a sledgehammer and sweeping
the spotlight into a dustpan,
when it's enough to say enough
and sit with your clown shoes curled.
When you lean your head back
after the last show, your eyelids shut,
not with the click of the kewpie
the little girl carries, but slowly
as with weights attached, tugging
your lashes to your painted face.
It's enough to sag with the hour of the day
in a sort of setting, not dying, or anything
so dramatic, but in repose, like the way
the limb of a large tree, an elm maybe,
exhales before the sun dips, the cicadas
erupting on cue and unrehearsed.
The air you breathe
is at once your own, and not your own,
and tomorrow will be, if not here,
then somewhere the same.

Cigar Box

Some cicadas take seventeen years
to emerge from below the sweet gum,
eggs on a delayed fuse, exploding
in a distant summer. Years ago, I found
an axe head in an Arkansas cave.
It took decades, guessing
from the rust, before it was returned
to the light. I own a metal detector
that I thought could sweep-up secrets
from city parks. One afternoon, I dug
an Indian head nickel, the date smoothed
and nearly unreadable. I imagined
it fell from the pocket of a boy
as he fisted a baseball card, or was juggled
by an old man before it flipped free
into the lawn. My grandson
found it again in a corner of a cigar box.
The night he was born
I brushed his cheek with my knuckle.

Acknowledgements

Atticus Review: "Grandma Goes Heavy"

Bards Against Hunger: Kansas: "Dust Jacket," "Stopping at Blackjack Camp after the Veteran's Writing Workshop," "Walking Under September Pines"

Beechwood Review: "Writing a Love Poem while the Plumber Snakes the Basement Drain"

By&By Poetry: "Goldfinch Burial"

Calamus Journal: "Growing Tomatoes"

Chiron Review: "In Search of Quivira We Found Chicken Fried Rice," "Peeing at McDonald's After Eating a Chicken Sandwich," "Tying Flies"

Coal City Review: "First Walk in the Rain after Retirement," "Mexicans Cutting Trees"

Diode: "Choosing the Five-Year Battery," "Green Tara"

Eunoia Review: "Dogs Have Changed," "Guilt Trip," "Pharmacy Run," "Two Truths About Fishing"

Drunk Monkeys: "Death of the Machinist's Mate"

Front Porch Review: "Interrupting the Artist"

great weather for MEDIA: "One-Star Toenail"

Hamilton Stone Review: "Five-Dollar Horn"

I-70 Review: "Bad Eye," "Continental Drift," "Stand-Up Cat," "Watching the Lunar Landing on Television while Taking Tickets at the Drive-In Theater"

In Between Hangovers: "Coffee Tonight"

Konza: "Caught Naked with Her," "Suffering on the Floor of a Fast Food Bathroom Stall I Imagine Amerigo Vespucci," "Weekenders"

The Long Islander (Whitman's Corner): "Watching the Solar Eclipse in the Rain"

Long Island Quarterly: "No Phil Rizzuto"

The Penn Review: "Cigar Box"

Poetry Bay: "Creeping South," "Keeping the Stetson," "Packing-Up the Classroom," "Smudge Pots," "Topeka Tornado 1966"

Rattle: "Butterfly Valve," "The Taco Boat"

Rattle Poets Respond: "The Senate Vows Impartial Justice"

Red Eft Review: "Ashes," "Cow Creek Snow," "DNA," "What We Keep"

Riggwelter: "Taking the Chipmunk Seriously"

Rust + Moth: "Carp," "Signature Piece"

The Shining Years: "Alf Considers the Next Big Thing," "Alf Chooses the Cherry Pie," "Alf Works the South Hallway"

Softblow: "Abbey Raises Chickens," "Of an Evening," "slicing the five o'clock cake"

Star 82 Review: "Flying Over the Coast of Greenland"

Turtle Island Quarterly: "Good Friday," "November Faces"

Up the Staircase Quarterly: "I Make a Joke about Equanimity at the Waffle House"

Valparaiso Poetry Review: "Saturday at the Pawn Shop," "The Sleep of Emmett Kelly"

Your One Phone Call: "Polio Turtle"